WHY YOU DON'T FEEL GOD

Entering the Secret of the Lord

By D.A. Cook

I0201532

Copyright © 2025 D. A. Cook

All rights reserved.

No part of this book may be reproduced, distributed, or transmitted in any form or by any means, including photocopying, recording, or other electronic or mechanical methods, without the prior written permission of the publisher, except in the case of brief quotations embodied in critical reviews and certain other noncommercial uses permitted by copyright law.

Published by Bring Back the Fire Publishing

ISBN: 978-0-9851820-2-1

Printed in the United States of America

"Whoever loses his life for my sake will find it."
— *Jesus (Matthew 16:25)*

INTRODUCTION
Why You Feel Nothing

You have been lied to. Not by atheists. Not by scientists. Not even by the culture wars everyone is screaming about. You were lied to by the people who told you that you are the answer.

The entire self-help industrial complex has sold the same message in different packaging. Every manifestation guru. Every "look within" prophet. Every polished voice promising that the universe bends to your intention. They all say the same thing: you do not need God, you need to become Him. And we believed it. All of us did.

Here is what they never tell you. The Secret did not sell over thirty-five million copies because it denied God existed. It sold because it offered something that sounded better than God: control. Think about it. What sounds more appealing, waiting on an invisible God who moves on His own timeline, or manifesting the life you want through the power of your thoughts right now? One requires humility, patience, and trust. The other requires a vision board and good vibes. We did not abandon God. We reduced Him. We turned Him into a cosmic vending machine and promoted ourselves to management.

You say you believe in God, but you do not feel Him. That makes sense. You have been trained to treat spirituality like a performance review, a system where God is evaluated based on whether He showed up the way you expected. But Scripture never promised that God would make you feel spiritual. It promised something far better. God came to save you from the exhausting lie that you can save yourself. That sentence is the reason this book exists.

If you are tired, burned out from trying to positive-think your way into peace, worn down from pretending you have everything under control, then you are exactly where David was when he wrote Psalm 25.

David was not a manifestation teacher. He was a king surrounded by enemies, burdened by his own failures, leading a nation always one decision away from disaster. When he prayed, he did not ask God to affirm his emotions. He prayed, "Lead me in Thy truth, and teach me: for Thou art the God of my salvation; on Thee do I wait all the day." Read that again. "On Thee do I wait." Not I claim. Not I manifest. Not I speak into existence. I wait.

That is the secret nobody wants to sell you. Waiting does not feel powerful. Surrender does not fit on a motivational post. Dependence does not sell books. But it does something manifestation never will. It works.

Here is the truth stated plainly. You cannot have God as your Savior while you are sitting as judge over Him. A judge evaluates. A judge withholds approval. A judge decides what is acceptable. And as long as you are assessing God's presence based on how you feel, you are not surrendering. You are auditing. Salvation does not begin with a feeling. It begins when you stop pretending you are in charge.

This book is not about learning how to feel God more. It is about unlearning the lie that taught you to replace Him. Psalm 25 is not emotional. It is positional. Your position matters more than your feelings ever will. Whether you are standing as judge or kneeling as student changes everything.

If you are exhausted, if you are done carrying the weight of trying to manage your own life, if you are willing to consider that the secret was never about unlocking your inner power, then turn the page. The real secret has been here all along. And once you see it, nothing stays the same.

THE LIE WE INHERITED
When We Made Ourselves the Source

The problem never started with disbelief. It started with confidence. Not the steady confidence that anchors a soul, but the arrogant kind that quietly replaces God. It began as a whisper that the deepest answers lie inside us. It told us that if we just dig deeper, manifest more, and know ourselves better, we could achieve the life of our dreams.

This lie shows up in schools, churches, therapy offices, podcasts, and books. It comes across as helpful and even wise, but it quietly changes people's focus from God to themselves.

Humanity's story has never been about whether we believe in something greater. Nearly everyone does. The real story is about misplaced trust. Where we place it, what we entrust it to, and how quickly we shift the line when dependence feels weak.

We learned early that control feels smarter than surrender. We built cultures on it. Productivity became virtue. Insight became authority. Feelings became proof. And truth became flexible, elastic enough to bless whatever we chose.

The shift was subtle. We stopped asking what is true. We started asking what feels true to me. We called it progress. It was a regression.

We are replaying the oldest story. The first one.

Take and eat. Your eyes will be opened. You will be like God, knowing good and evil.

The words change, but the tone never does. It still whispers that you are wise enough now. That you can define good for yourself. That you know yourself better than anyone, better than Him.

You feel the pull, don't you? The tension between reverence and self-definition. The urge to curate the sacred, to keep what aligns and discard what offends. To trust your own moral compass over the One who made the stars.

Self-knowledge feels dignified. Dependence feels childish.

Yet every generation discovers the same brutal truth. When the self claims God's throne, the weight crushes.

Slowly, you notice your mind filled with advice from social media, your heart feeling restless, and your days packed with tasks. Still, when you climb into bed, you feel a quiet emptiness.

That hollow is not failure. It is evidence. Something in us still remembers that we were never meant to be the final source.

The lie promised independence. It delivered ache. It promised enlightenment. It dimmed the light until all we saw was our own reflection.

Faith has not vanished. It has only changed direction. We still believe every day, in our instincts, our intuition, our curated truths.

What we have truly lost is dependence on God, the central shift that underlies our struggles and disconnection.

Trusting God instead of yourself may seem old-fashioned or risky, but it is the only way people find real hope and clarity.

WHEN FAITH BECAME A FEELING
The Myth that Emotions Prove God's Presence

Dependence asks us to trust what we cannot always feel. That is exactly why we traded it away. We made faith a matter of sensation instead of substance. If God is near, we assume we should feel warmth. If He is speaking, the words should land with electricity. If He loves us, the heart should hum with certainty. But true faith is not a feeling. It is anchored dependence on God regardless of our senses. This is the quiet disaster of our age: we turned the presence of God into a feeling.

The Bible never promised constant emotion. It does promise constant truth.

Abraham waited decades for a son and received silence more often than signs. David wrote psalms drenched in despair, yet he never questioned the covenant. Jesus Himself cried out in forsakenness on the cross and still finished the work. None of them measured God's nearness by how they felt in the moment. They measured it by what He had already declared.

We reversed the order.

Now experience leads, and truth must follow. If we feel distant, God must be distant. If we feel empty, the Spirit must have left. If we feel nothing, faith must be failing.

Feelings are fickle: they rise with good coffee, fall with bad sleep, and vanish in hospital waiting rooms. They are weather, not foundation, yet we've been taught to treat them as proof.

Modern spirituality tells us to listen to our heart. Scripture says the heart is deceitful above all things. The difference is not small.

When faith becomes a feeling, dependence becomes optional. We lean on God only when leaning feels good. When it does not, we reach for the next technique, the next conference, the next emotional reset. The result is a generation of believers perpetually chasing the next high and perpetually afraid of ordinary silence.

But God is not always in the wind, the earthquake, or the fire. He is often in the still small voice that speaks truth, whether we tremble or not. Real faith returns to that voice. It says, I will trust what You said, even when I feel nothing.

It chooses the anchor of Scripture over the tides of emotion. Dependence is not expecting fireworks; it is stepping forward in faith because God's promise holds, not our feelings.

The moment we stop requiring God to prove Himself through feeling, something remarkable happens. The pressure lifts. The performance ends. We are free to be honest about our emptiness without fearing it disqualifies us. And in that honesty, the real light begins to return, not as a rush, but as a steady presence we no longer have to earn.

THE WEIGHT WE CARRY
The Real-Life Cost of Being Your Own God

When faith becomes a feeling and dependence feels optional, we end up carrying what was never meant to rest on our shoulders. The symptoms arrive slowly, disguised as normal life. We label them stress, burnout, and dryness. We compare ourselves to others. But these are the consequences of choosing to sit where only God belongs.

First comes performance. Every quiet moment must be filled with productivity or prayer that feels right. Silence becomes suspicious. Rest feels like laziness. We begin grading ourselves by how inspired we were today, how close we felt, and how much we accomplished for the kingdom.

Then comparison creeps in. We scroll through other people's highlight reels of breakthroughs, anointings, and answered prayers. Their fire makes our embers look like failure. So we push harder, pray longer, confess more, and chase the emotion they seem to have.

Anxiety follows close behind. If God's nearness depends on our effort, then any slip means He might leave. We live in low-grade dread.

What if I am not doing enough?
What if my faith is too small?
What if this dry season means I have been disqualified?

Am I even saved at all?
Am I chosen?

The body keeps score. Sleepless nights. A tight chest. Racing thoughts at three in the morning. Spiritual fatigue that no amount of worship playlists can fix. We mistake the exhaustion for devotion. We wear it like a badge. I am pressing in.

But the deepest weight is shame. When the self is god, every unanswered prayer, every flat season, every moment of doubt becomes a personal indictment. We do not just feel distant from God. We feel we have failed Him. We have let Him down. We are the problem.

This is the cruel irony of self-reliance. It promises freedom from external rules but installs an internal judge far stricter than any law. The old covenant at least gave us a standard we could see. The new religion of self gives us a mirror we can never satisfy.

And in the quiet, when the striving finally pauses, the ache speaks clearly. This is too heavy. I was not built to carry my own salvation.

The good news is that the weight is not proof of our failure. It is proof of our design. We were made to depend, not to self-sustain. The crushing load is the body crying out for what it was created to do, to lean.

God does not scold us for buckling under the burden. He waits for us to drop it at His feet. Because the moment we stop trying to be our own savior, the shoulders that have always been strong enough become available again.

THE BIBLICAL ANTIDOTE
Dependence Was Always the Plan

The weight we carry is not a sign that we are broken. It is a sign that we are finally waking up to the truth God has been saying from the beginning. You were never designed to stand alone.

Scripture does not present dependence as a fallback plan for the weak. It presents dependence as the original blueprint for the strong.

Look at Abraham. God promised him a son and then waited twenty-five years to deliver. In the silence, Abraham tried to manufacture the promise himself. Ishmael was the result. The pain that followed lasted generations. When Abraham finally stopped striving, God spoke clearly. "I am your shield; your reward shall be very great" (Genesis 15:1). The promise did not come through effort. It came through surrender.

Look at David. In a cave, hunted by Saul and surrounded by enemies, he wrote, "My soul waits for the Lord more than watchmen for the morning" (Psalm 130:6). He did not pray for quicker escape. He prayed for strength to wait. Dependence was his weapon.

Look at Jesus. In Gethsemane, He did not rally His willpower. He fell on His face and said, "Not my will, but yours be done" (Luke 22:42). The Son of God modeled perfect dependence, not because He was limited, but because dependence is the nature of true relationship with the Father.

Paul seals it. After pleading three times for the thorn to be removed, he heard the answer, "My grace is sufficient for you, for my power is made perfect in weakness" (2 Corinthians 12:9). Paul's conclusion was unmistakable. "I will boast all the more gladly of my weaknesses, so that the power of Christ may rest upon me."

Weakness was not the problem. Self-sufficiency was.

The Bible never hides the cost of dependence. It costs pride. It costs control. It costs the illusion that we can fix ourselves. But it also gives what self-effort never could. Rest. Peace that does not depend on circumstances. Strength that comes from outside us.

Every attempt to outgrow dependence is a rerun of the Garden. Every return to dependence is a return to Eden's posture, walking with God in the cool of the day, hand in hand, trusting Him for what we cannot provide.

This is not regression. This is recovery.

The antidote was written into the story from the first page. "Trust in the Lord with all your heart, and do not lean on your own understanding" (Proverbs 3:5). The Hebrew word for lean is the same word used for resting your full weight on something.

God is inviting us to rest our full weight on Him, not occasionally, not when we feel strong enough, but always. When we do, the shoulders that have carried the impossible become the shoulders we finally let carry us.

MYTH: EMOTION AS EVIDENCE
Truth Must Lead, Not Follow Our Feelings

We have made God's nearness a matter of mood. If the heart sings, He is close. If it is silent, He must have withdrawn. This myth is seductive because it feels personal. We want to know God is real, so we look inside for confirmation.

When the warmth of worship arrives, we celebrate. When the warmth vanishes in the ordinary, we panic. The panic is real. Many believers live with a low-grade fear. What if I am not feeling enough? What if my dryness means I have drifted too far? What if God is waiting for a better version of me before He returns?

David knew this fear intimately. In Psalm 25, he lifts his soul to God and pleads, "I trust in you; do not let me be put to shame." He admits loneliness, affliction, troubles enlarged, enemies fierce. Yet he anchors himself in God's character, not his own emotional state. "Guide me in your truth and teach me, for you are God my Savior, and my hope is in you all day long."

David does not demand fireworks. He asks for truth to lead. He waits all day, eyes fixed on the Lord, even when his soul feels trapped in a net.

We have forgotten that lesson. We treat emotion as the final judge. A dry season means God is distant. Tears in prayer mean God is near. The result is a faith that rises and falls with the weather of the heart.

Scripture tells a different story. Truth stands firm when feelings falter. God promises presence based on His word, not our feelings. "Be strong and courageous. Do not be afraid; do not be discouraged, for the Lord your God will be with you wherever you go" (Joshua 1:9). That promise was not conditional on how Joshua felt that day.

When we let emotion lead, dependence becomes sporadic. We lean only when leaning feels good. We trust only when trust feels secure. We wait only when waiting feels hopeful. But dependence is not about feeling secure. It is about choosing the secure One when nothing feels secure.

The myth collapses under its own weight. Feelings are not proof. They are passengers. They come and go, rise and fall, whisper and shout. Truth is the driver. When we let truth take the wheel, emotions can finally ride along without dictating the destination.

David models this in Psalm 25. He pours out shame, cries for relief from distress, and confesses great guilt. Yet he declares, "None who wait for you will be put to shame." He does not wait for the shame to lift before trusting. He trusts in the midst of shame, and the waiting becomes the path to freedom.

This is the invitation. Stop monitoring your internal temperature. Start standing on what God has said. Let truth lead, and experience will follow, sometimes with feeling and sometimes without. Either way, the presence is real because the promise is sure.

The moment we release emotion as evidence, the pressure to perform lifts. We can be honest about dryness without fear of disqualification. We can wait without panic. We can depend without demanding proof. And in that quiet shift, the real light returns, steady, not as a rush we must chase, but as a presence we were never meant to earn.

THE PRACTICE OF WAITING
Where Real Rest Begins

Waiting is not passive. It is the active choice to stop striving and start depending. Most of us have been trained to hate waiting. We fill every gap with noise, plans, or self-talk. Silence feels like wasted time. Stillness feels like surrender to defeat.

But Scripture calls waiting a holy act. Isaiah heard God say, "In returning and rest you shall be saved; in quietness and in trust shall be your strength" (Isaiah 30:15). The Hebrew word for "wait" in Psalm 25 is qavah, which means to bind together, to twist, and to hope expectantly. David does not sit idly. He actively twists his soul toward God when he says, "I wait for you all day long."

This waiting is not empty. It is full of intention. It is the soul saying, "I will not manufacture the answer. I will not force the feeling. I will hold my place and trust You to move."

Waiting becomes real through simple, embodied practices in everyday life. The first is creating space for silence. Start small. Five minutes in the morning or evening with no phone, no music, and no agenda. Just sit and breathe. Let the mind wander and then gently return to one line of truth, "You are God my Savior" (Psalm 25:5). When distraction comes, and it will, do not fight it. Name it and release it. The goal is not perfect focus. The goal is honest presence.

The second practice is praying the prayer of surrender. David models this in Psalm 25, saying, "Show me your ways, Lord, teach me your paths." Use those words or your own. "Lord, I do not know what today holds. I do not feel You. But I lift my soul to You. Guide me. Teach me. I wait on You." Say it out loud if possible. The voice helps the heart remember.

The third practice is anchoring in Scripture instead of self-talk. When the inner voice says, "You are not doing enough," or "God has gone quiet because you are failing," respond with truth. Repeat Psalm 25:21, "May integrity and uprightness protect me, because my hope is in you." Not your performance. Not your feelings. Your hope is in Him.

The fourth practice is micro waiting throughout the day. In line at the store. In traffic. Before opening your inbox. Pause for ten seconds and whisper, "I wait for you, Lord." These small pauses retrain the soul to lean instead of lunge.

The fifth practice is confessing the need for control. When anxiety spikes, name it. "I am trying to be my own god again." Then release it. "Forgive me. I lay this down. I depend on You." Confession is not punishment. It is freedom.

Waiting will feel awkward at first. The soul has been trained to produce, not to receive. But the awkwardness is the sign of change. The more you wait, the more you discover that God is already present in the silence. He does not need our noise to speak. He does not need our feelings to be near.

David waited in caves, in exile, and in the shadow of death. He waited with enemies, with guilt, and with loneliness. And he still declared, "None who wait for you will be put to shame" (Psalm 25:3).

Waiting is not a delay. It is dependence in motion. It is the soul twisting toward the only One who never moves away. When we practice this, rest arrives. Not as a feeling we chase, but as a reality we receive. The weight lifts because we have stopped carrying what was never ours to hold.

LEANING IN
The Daily Mechanics of Dependence

Dependence is not a one-time decision. It is a daily posture. It is a thousand small choices to lean instead of lunge. The soul that has tasted rest begins to crave it, but old habits die slowly. The mind still races to fix. The heart still hunts for feeling. The hands still grasp for control. These practices retrain the soul to stay leaned in, moment by moment.

Begin each day with a soul lift. David opens Psalm 25 with the words, "To you, O Lord, I lift up my soul." Do the same. Before the phone, before the to do list, speak it aloud. "Lord, I lift my soul to You today. Everything in me, the fear, the hope, the noise, the quiet, I place in Your hands." This simple act disarms the illusion that you must carry yourself.

Use Scripture as your daily anchor. Choose one verse to carry through the day. Psalm 25:5 works beautifully. "Guide me in your truth and teach me, for you are God my Savior, and my hope is in you all day long." Write it on a card, set it as your lock screen, whisper it in the car. When self-doubt or anxiety speaks, answer with the verse. Truth crowds out the lie.

Practice confession as a rhythm. When you catch yourself striving, micromanaging outcomes, chasing approval, forcing answers, pause and confess. "I am trying to be my own god again. Forgive me. I depend on You." Confession is not defeat.

It is the quickest way back to dependence. It clears the clutter and returns you to the posture of a child.

Build in pauses of remembrance. Three times a day, morning, midday, and evening, stop for thirty seconds. Ask yourself, "What am I carrying that is not mine?" Then release it. "I give this to You." These pauses become the hinges of the day. They remind the soul that God is holding what you cannot.

Surround yourself with reminders of grace. Community matters. Find people who talk about dependence on Christ, not performance. Listen to music that lifts truth, not just emotion. Read stories of saints who waited well. These voices echo the prayer of Psalm 25, "Remember, O Lord, your great mercy and love, for they are from of old." They keep the heart oriented when feelings fail.

End the day in gratitude and trust. Before sleep, name one thing you did not control today and thank God for holding it. Then borrow David's closing words, "Redeem Israel, O God, out of all their troubles" (Psalm 25:22). Replace Israel with your own name, your family, or your situation. It becomes a final act of dependence. "I leave this with You."

These practices are not new rules to master. They are gentle invitations to keep leaning. You will forget. You will slip back into striving. That is normal. Dependence does not require perfection. It requires continuous return.

Each time you return, the posture strengthens. The soul learns that leaning is safer than standing alone. The weight stays lighter because you are no longer the one holding it.

David waited all day long, eyes on the Lord, soul lifted, hope fixed. He was not superhuman. He was dependent. And dependence turned a hunted king into a man after God's own heart.

The same path is open to us. Not as a formula, but as a relationship. Lean in today. Lean again tomorrow. The God who never moves away will meet you every time.

FREEDOM ON THE OTHER SIDE
What Dependence Actually Feels Like

When the striving finally stops, something unexpected happens. You do not arrive at a constant emotional high. You arrive at something quieter, deeper, and far more stable. You arrive at freedom from being your own god.

This freedom does not feel like fireworks. It feels like putting down a backpack you did not realize you were carrying for years. The shoulders ache less. Breathing comes easier. The constant inner judge quiets down. You are no longer grading your faith by how inspired you felt today. You are no longer scanning your emotions for proof that God is still there. You are no longer afraid that dryness means disqualification.

The lie was this. If you just believe hard enough in yourself, manifest clearly enough, get your heart right, God will respond. That was starvation. You were eating your own performance and wondering why you stayed hungry.

The truth is simpler and harder. You were never supposed to feed yourself.

Dependence means letting God be the source. Not once a week in a good service. Not only when you feel broken enough. Every day. All day. Even when you feel nothing.

What does that actually feel like? It feels like permission to be honest. You can say out loud, "I do not feel You today," without panic. You can admit doubt, guilt, or fear without thinking it cancels the relationship.

David did this constantly in Psalm 25. He lifted his soul to God while still confessing shame, enemies, and loneliness. He did not wait until he felt holy to trust. He trusted because God is faithful, not because David was.

It feels like the end of the performance. You stop auditioning for God's approval. You stop measuring your worth by how on fire you are. You stop comparing your quiet season to someone else's breakthrough. The inner scorecard shuts off. Not because you have arrived, but because you have stopped trying to arrive.

It feels like rest that does not depend on circumstances. Trouble still comes. Dryness still happens. Questions still linger. But the terror that this means God left is gone. You know He has not. He promised. You lean on the promise, not the feeling.

It feels like being small again, and that is not weakness. It is reality. You are not God. You never were. Admitting that is not defeat. It is the door to real strength, His strength, not yours.

Most of all, it feels like coming home. Not to a perfect version of yourself. Not to a life without pain. But to the One who has been waiting the whole time. No lecture. No, I told you so. Just open arms for the child who finally stopped running.

This is freedom on the other side. Not euphoria. Not invincibility. Just the simple, steady relief of no longer carrying what was crushing you.

You did not miss something. You were told a lie. The lie kept you starving. The truth feeds you.

And the truth is this. God has not moved. He is still the Savior. He is still faithful. You can lean your full weight on Him. Right now. Today. Tomorrow. Always.

FOR THE TIRED BELIEVER
When You've Already Tried Everything

You are exhausted. You have read the books. You have prayed the prayers. You have declared, confessed, visualized, journaled, fasted, served, and repented harder. You chased the breakthrough. You tried to believe bigger, feel deeper, manifest clearer. And you are still tired.

The emptiness did not leave. The closeness did not arrive. The peace did not settle. Now you are afraid you missed something. Maybe you did not have enough faith. Maybe your heart was not pure enough. Maybe God is waiting for you to get it right one more time.

Listen carefully. You did not miss something. You were fed a lie.

The lie said peace is something you produce. God's presence is something you earn. Rest is the reward for your performance. That is not the gospel. That is starvation dressed as spirituality.

You have been trying to save yourself with better self-faith. Every technique, every emotional high, every step of faith was still you trying to be the source. No wonder you are weary. No one can carry their own salvation. No one can keep themselves close to God by effort.

The truth is simpler, and it stings at first because it feels too good to be true. God is not waiting for you to get it right. He is waiting for you to stop trying to get it right. He is not measuring your worth by how much you have accomplished in the spiritual gym. He is not grading your closeness by how consistently you feel Him. He is not withholding Himself until you prove you deserve Him.

He is already there. He has never left.

The distance you feel is not His withdrawal. It is the weight you are carrying that He promised to carry.

Stop. Drop it.

You do not need another method. You need one posture. Dependence.

Dependence looks like this. "I am tired. I have tried everything. I cannot fix this. I lift my soul to You anyway. You are God, my Savior. My hope is in You."

That is enough.

It was enough for David in Psalm 25 when he was surrounded by enemies, drowning in shame, and still said, "In you I trust; do not let me be put to shame." He did not wait until he felt strong. He trusted in the middle of weakness.

You can do the same. Right now. No prerequisites. No perfect heart required. Just the honest admission, "I am done striving. I depend on You."

The tiredness is not a sign of failure. It is a sign that you have been running on the wrong fuel. Self faith burns out fast. Dependence on God is the only thing that sustains.

You are not disqualified. You are not behind. You are not forgotten.

You are exactly where God meets people. At the end of their rope. At the bottom of their trying.

Let the striving die. Let the performance end. Let the fear that you missed the secret fade.

The secret was never inside you. It was always Him.

And He is still here. Still faithful. Still willing to carry what you cannot.

Just lean.

That is all.
That is everything.

FOR THE SKEPTICAL SEEKER
If God is Real, Why the Silence?

You are not sure if there is anyone out there. Or if there is, you are not convinced He cares. Or if He cares, you are not sure He is listening to you. That is fair. You have seen too many empty promises. Too many people claim God speaks through feelings, signs, or coincidences that never come. Too many times, you have whispered into the dark and heard nothing back.

The silence hurts. It makes you suspicious. It makes you wonder if the whole thing is just humans talking to themselves, inventing comfort because the quiet is too loud.

Here is the plain truth. The silence is not proof that God is not there. It is proof that we have been looking for Him in the wrong place.

Most of us begin with the same default, self-faith. We trust our own reasoning, our own feelings, our own ability to figure life out. We ask questions like, 'Does this make sense to me? Does this feel right? Do I like this version of truth?' When the answers do not satisfy, we conclude there is nothing out there. Or worse, that if there is, He is not worth knowing.

But self-faith has already failed you. You tried to be your own compass and ended up lost. You tried to be your own comfort and ended up empty. You tried to be your own answer and ended up more tired and more alone.

That failure is not the end of the story. It is the beginning of honesty.

Dependence begins where self-faith ends, with the admission that you do not have all the answers. That your heart can deceive you. That your mind can trick you. You are limited, finite, and not the center of the universe. That admission is not weakness. It is the most honest thing a human can do.

Once you are there, you can ask a different question. Not, do I feel God? Not, does this prove He exists? But a simpler one. If You are real, and if You are listening, show me. I am done pretending I can do this alone. I am open.

That is dependence in its rawest form. No formula. No religious performance. No requirement to feel anything first. Just the quiet choice to stop running the show and leave the door cracked open.

David did this in Psalm 25. He was not a theologian writing a treatise. He was a man in trouble, surrounded by enemies, full of shame, and he said, "To you, O Lord, I lift up my soul." He did not wait until he felt sure. He did not wait until the evidence was overwhelming. He lifted what he had, doubts and all, and trusted that if God was real, He would meet him there.

You can do the same. You do not have to clean up your doubts first. You do not have to manufacture faith. You do not have to pretend you believe more than you do.

Just say it. Out loud if you can. In the car, in the shower, in the dark. "If You are there, I am here. I am tired of being my own god. I am willing to depend on You instead. Show me who You are."

The silence may continue for a while. God is not a vending machine. He does not owe us immediate proof. But the silence is not abandonment. It is often the space where real trust is born.

When self-faith finally crumbles, when you stop demanding proof on your terms, something shifts. The quiet becomes less threatening. The possibility becomes more interesting.

And if God is who He says He is, the God who made you, who knows you, who has never stopped loving you, He will meet you in that honest place. Not because you earned it. Not because you felt enough. But because He is faithful.

You have not missed the secret. The secret was never hidden. It was buried under the noise of trying to save yourself.

Take the small step. Lift your soul. Leave the door open.

That is all He needs.

CONCLUSION
The Secret That Was Never Hidden

The secret you were told to find inside yourself was never there. It was never meant to be. You were told the answers were in your heart, your intuition, your self-knowledge, your faith level. You were told to dig deeper, believe harder, manifest clearer, and become your own light.

You tried and you exhausted yourself searching for what was promised but never delivered. That was the lie. The lie that turned dependence into something childish and self-faith into something noble. The lie that made you the source instead of the receiver. The lie that left you starving while pretending you were feasting.

The real secret was never hidden. It was spoken plainly from the beginning. It was lived out in every person who dared to lean when everything in them wanted to stand alone. It was written in the pages you already know. Trust in the Lord with all your heart and do not lean on your own understanding. Wait for the Lord, be strong, and let your heart take courage. To you, O Lord, I lift up my soul.

This is not a new revelation. It is the oldest invitation. The one that has been waiting for you the whole time you were busy trying to save yourself.

You do not need more effort. You do not need a better version of yourself. You do not need to feel more, pray more perfectly, or prove more worthiness. You need only to stop and drop the weight you were never meant to carry. To lift your soul to the One who has been holding it all along.

He is not distant because you failed. He is not silent because you doubted. He is not gone because you tried too hard. He is the God who made you. He knows every crack in your heart, every hidden shame, every weary question.

And He is still here. Still faithful. Still saying, come. Lean. Rest. Depend.

The posture is simple. I cannot. You can. I trust You.

That is enough. It always has been.

Now the quiet begins. Not the empty quiet of abandonment, but the full quiet of being known and held. The space where you no longer have to perform, produce, or pretend.

The invitation stands. It has never changed. It will not change.

Lift your soul. Leave the door open. Lean your full weight.

He has been waiting to meet you right there.

You are not forgotten. You are not disqualified. You are exactly where grace finds people. At the end of trying. At the beginning of dependence.

And that is where real life begins.

www.ingramcontent.com/pod-product-compliance
Lightning Source LLC
Chambersburg PA
CBHW021148020426
42331CB00005B/957